Herstorys

Herstorys

– HER HISTORY TOLD THROUGH THE EYES OF HER TRUE SELF. –

Nyeesha D. Williams

Copyright © 2015 Authored By Mrs. Nyeesha D. Williams
All rights reserved.

ISBN: 0692386505
ISBN 13: 9780692386507
Library of Congress Control Number: 2015902710
Nyeesha D. Williams ,Canoga Park, CA

Dedication

*To my husband, my two daughters, my parents, and my sisters.
Also to my Sacrit Devas and my team in Kampala, Uganda.*

*Thank you all. Without your support and patience,
I never would have achieved this dream.*

Table of Contents

Naked

RIP	2
Distraction	4
Harmless	6
Disney	8
Rhythmic Sound of Hell	10
Open	12
No Payment	14
Not Such a Team Player	16
Thanks, Stranger	18
Ballerina Blues	20
True Love	22
Cured from Trust	24
Harmonious Tears	26
Abused Power	28
Bitch	30
Pregnancy Pact	32
Who Is Laughing?	34
Poor Son	36
The Nurturing Woman	38
The Test	40
My Man That Got Away	42

Revelations · 44
Plantation · 46
Three Wise Men · 48
She · 50
Slut · 52
Love · 54
Ghost of Childhood Past · · · · · · · · · · · · · · · 56
Early-Wedding Blues · · · · · · · · · · · · · · · · · 58
As I Lay · 60
Suicidal Attempts · 62
Life on Repeat · 64
His Mother · 66
Green Street · 68
Date Rape · 70
Marriage · 72

Transformation

Sacrit · 76
Soul Cry · 78
Perspectives · 80
Feminist · 82
Duty · 84
S & S · 86
Her · 88
S & P · 90

Affirmations

Truth · 102
Beauty · 104
Peace · 106
Fear · 108

Pain · 110
Growth · 112
Love · 114
Sisterhood · 116

Acknowledgments

I would like to thank Ms. Tucker from Union Avenue Middle School. May she rest in peace. As I always promised her, I will acknowledge her forever. I also would like to thank my mommy, one of the strongest women I know. Your ability to continue pressing on no matter the circumstances allowed me to see you as the true diamond that you are.

To my oldest daughter, Zani'yah: you've always been my rock and my savior. When it seemed as if Mommy didn't care, here is my proof that you were always my reason to hold on. To my youngest born, Melody: you came into my life at the right time. When I got out of control and believed there was no other way, you appeared. To my stepfather, whom I always love as my very own: you rock, but your football team still sucks! I love you.

To all the board members, partners, contractors, and volunteers at Sacrit Devahood Incorporation: You all have supported me and this mission like no one else and have seen in me what I could not see in myself. This act of love never will be forgotten, and you'll forever be in my heart. To my dear James: you have watched me grow and, even with all of my faults, never loved me less. You are the essence of a true friend. I will forever love you with my heart and soul.

To my teammate, my headache, my partner in crime, and my lover of all lovers: my husband. I am you; you are I; and these reflections are looking pretty damn good! Thank you for your patience, guidance, and use of the editor's red pen.

Introduction

I want to begin this journey with truth, truth within myself, and also gain trust from you. I want to build a relationship between us and form a true sisterhood. I want to personally thank you for your donation. You officially have deposited a wealth into my life like no other. For you to take the time out to even grab hold of this book says a lot. As we walk this road together, I ask that you be as honest with me as possible. Open all your senses your entire soul and while you're at it, grab a pen or pencil.

I am officially your keeper, as you are mine. In each entry I have expressed my thoughts, stories, and confessions to you. I've done this because I believe in being transparent. I beg for you to do the same with me. Talk back to me (you are *not* crazy), tell me what you feel each time you finish reading one of the entries. When you begin writing, be truthful with yourself and to me. Whatever emotions are present, just *feel them*. If what I've written brings back old memories, if you hate me at the moment, or even if you have that "aha" moment that Oprah talks about all the time, *tell me.*

As you'll notice while reading this book, my attitude will change. You'll get to understand me as a woman and see that my life went from one direction to another.

I am you.

We are one.

I've overcome many of life's challenges and found a way to happiness. I found the meaning of being a true sister's keeper. I found the meaning of forgiveness, and I live it. Consider this our shared diary, and you're the only one with the key (unless you show me where it is).

Join me.

Naked

RIP

He was my favorite.
My daddy's brother is what they considered him. I always loved to see him smile because I knew my face would look the same as his almost immediately. We would go into the bedroom with two twin beds and this barrel-looking thingy. I would sit on one bed, and he always took the other. We laughed and joked over the long white lines that he created with such a fast chopping technique. I screamed so loud with laughter and nasal pain. Nothing was ever better than the two combined.

Distraction

He was so cute.
He stood tall and brown skinned. His shoulders started from South America and went to Asia. He looked to be some guy from one of those body-builder magazines.
He was so strong, poised, and lively.
This guy was definitely one of the coolest people I'd ever met. He was very protective and nice, but something about him was so wrong. He was the distraction from my mother's hand buying her dope.

Harmless

I found refuge under his sweaty body.
His sweat dripped all over my childish skin.
I knew that in order to feel safe from him, I had to act
as if what he was doing to me was harmless.

Disney

As he wrapped my favorite Mickey belt around his fragile arm, I knew it was time for me to head to bed. There was an unspoken understanding between us. The sickness he injected into his body was my way of knowing what time it was in the real world. The moment I saw his head go back was the moment my head rested on my pillow.
Good night, Mickey!

Rhythmic Sound of Hell

I lay on this cold bed with several silver instruments placed beside me.
I told myself they were clean, sterilized right before he met me here in this
empty place. I heard the music of childlike spirits, which became harmonious
to the beat of that one instrument scraping the wombs of so many women.
Dr. Him told me to close my eyes and count to three.
He stopped the music at two.

Open

He told me he loved me.
The only way I knew how to express my feelings for him was to unlock.
"Open wide…"
Opening wide with my legs, opening wide with my mouth,
opening wide with my soul.
He told me he loved me.
I lay there open as he closed the door.

No Payment

I walked into work.
He took me home, but he never paid me for that day's labor.

Not Such a Team Player

From my dad's house to my mother's home,
it was as if a game of checkers were being played.
He made it so much fun and strategized so well to the point that I didn't even
notice he was playing me.

Thanks, Stranger

The only generational curse I remember with this family was rape. This uncle raped that uncle; that niece raped that brother; and that brother raped that cousin. I guess I'm the special one. I had the pleasure of being raped by a relative and a stranger on the same night.

Ballerina Blues

I sat on the floor, so excited about class.
I had my leotard and tights on and was waiting to strap on my pointe shoes. After my shoes were strapped, I wrapped my skirt around my waist, and I immediately was free from misery.
I sat on the bed, feeling anxious about class.
I had my panties and bra on. As I waited for him, he strapped on his own custom protection. As I continued to watch him, I twirled and wrapped my cover around my heated body and welcomed misery.

True Love

I had a major surgery at seventeen.
They pushed the stretcher so fast into this cold room. No one could hold my hand. My mama wasn't present; he wasn't there; and Daddy probably was fucking someone. What seemed to be the largest knife being sharpened was accompanied by a maniacal laugh from the angriest butcher alive. Everyone was screaming my name, but I never answered.
This room was filled with emotionless strangers.
They told me to calm down, breathe, lie flat, and not make matters worse. This operation could either save me or kill me. Didn't the surgeon realize I was still a baby? Didn't the doctor see the tears that dripped off my cheeks?
I had a major surgery at seventeen.
I delivered my first love.

Cured from Trust

I sat in the doctor's office, nervous as hell.
I couldn't stop tapping the chair, rocking back and forth, and biting my nails.
I knew better than to have allowed myself to get in this situation. We had been together for some time, so being here seemed so uncalled for.
We loved each other so much.
I didn't understand how love had gotten me in this predicament of being tested. She called me to the back room, looked at my chart, and handed me a white powdery substance.
I asked her what it was, and she replied, "In this cup is proof that you trusted him too much."

Harmonious Tears

She kept crying over and over, as if she knew it angered me.
I begged her to stop and take a nap for at least an hour. Mommy needed some rest, and school was in the morning. She continued to cry,
not even caring about what I had to do.
She cried again, and I shook her until we cried in unison.

Abused Power

He made me call him "Daddy."
He was such a selfish bastard!
If only he knew who his father was,
I would tell his ass he was the cause of all this.

Bitch

One guy screamed it over the phone.
Another called me that while I was crossing the street.
Two more during class.
They all wondered why it never bothered me. Little did the assholes know that my mother had desensitized me by calling me that my whole life.

Pregnancy Pact

It was the two of us.
We sent messages to each other subliminally and so silently. We felt the energy of each other wanting that unconditional love. We knew we couldn't give each other this type of love, and there was only one other way.
We walked down the high-school hallways, imagining the school being the hospital right up the street.
We held hands as if we were in the process of pushing our babies out of our tight, precious bodies.
We ran home and met back up at the township library four weeks later.

Who Is Laughing?

I laughed at her.
I watched her being played for a fool
I laughed even harder when I watched her struggle with her children, but nothing was funny at all when later I was in her shoes, and she had no struggles at all.

Poor Son

I blamed my dad.
My dad then blamed his dad.
His dad never met his dad,
but my son still sits here and waits to meet them all.

The Nurturing Woman

I gave to all who visited me.
I am the one whose shoulder you cried on,
who fought your battles when you didn't know how.
I am the one who cradled you in the night when
branches tapped your window.
I am the one who caressed your shoulders after a long day of work.
I gave to the ones who knew not where I lived.
I am the one who donated my life's earnings to many countries and people.
I am the nurturing woman whom no one took the time to nurture.

The Test

My grandmother always told me she loved me.
I never believed her, so I took it upon myself to test her on my birthday.
I lay in the hospital bed, holding my dead son in my arms. I just knew if I cried out, she would come running. I mean, why wouldn't she if she loved me?
I did just that----*cried*.
She proved to me her love was genuine-genuine bullshit She never came running through that door.

My Man That Got Away

I married a man but yearned for another.
I didn't do this because the man was bad for me but because the man
I wanted cradled me when I cried.
I mean, this man was so handsome, so charismatic,
so persuasive, and so wanted by many.
I married a man but couldn't please him the way he needed to be pleased--
not because I wasn't physically capable but because the other man I yearned for
never asked for me physically.
When I was around this man, I felt pure, so childlike, so innocent, so needed.
I married a man but wanted only my daddy.

Revelations

I cried in the dark because tears didn't exist that way.
I smiled while the lights were on because questions weren't asked that way.
One day I made a huge mistake, and all my truth was revealed.

Plantation

I should have been branded and stood in line with the rest of the animals.
I was in bondage, stuck between two electrical gates with no way to escape.
My master gave me scraps to eat and rubbed my back when I was obedient.
I looked at the sorrow in everyone's eyes and knew a change was coming soon.
I stood my ass up and climbed that gate while almost killing myself.
I found freedom on the other side.

Three Wise Men

The only three men who mattered to me were all in one room.
Only G-d could have allowed this to happen.
The youngest one lay dead in my arms.
The oldest smiled as if all the years he hadn't been there for me had been erased out my mind.
The middle one was just sitting there…frightened.
I'm still not sure whether it was the fear of the youngest lungs looking collapsed in his small frame or the fear of my finding out he loved someone else.

She

Sometimes I cry for my inner child.
I cry because she is so lost yet so found.
I cry because she is abandoned yet so claimed.
I cry because she is so weak yet so strong.
As I cry for her, she cries for that outer woman I portray myself to be.
She knows me very well.

Slut

I was a slut.
A slut in my own right!
See, society would have called my actions dirty and not ladylike,
but I saw it differently.
I saw something invigorating, empowering, and masterful.
I saw living this slutty life as a craft.
Not all women could do this.
I placed all bodies wherever I wanted them and had my way with them.
I was in control, a high commodity, a force to be reckoned with.
Some may have thought I was a fool, but this life made me strategic.
It made me a businesswoman.

Love

I used this word to my advantage.
All this word ever meant to me was "Make life more convenient for me."

Ghost of Childhood Past

They look so happy.
I can see them, but they can't see me. Just look at them!
Look at the father, the mother, and their children, seeming so pleasant and believable.
They show the ultimate illusion of a complete family.
Do the children know they have a big sister?
Does the mother know about her daughter-in-law?
Look at him, holding their hands and playing Ring around the Rosie.
Shit.
Look at me.
My hands are becoming flesh, and so are my arms. I am reaching for this family without my control.
I am visible.
He's looking over at me.
He knows who I am.
He has recognized me.
I am his spitting image.
I am his true family tree.
Don't they look clueless now? Confused? Should we even have done this?
We are scaring the children!
Look at her crying.
I hear her. "Daddy, what's wrong?" she asks.
I'm stuck...*save me*. My identity is no longer our secret.
I hear him respond.
"That's my daughter. I ignored her as if she never would appear again."

Early-Wedding Blues

I walked down the aisle in my beautiful white Cinderella gown.
As the organ played its tune, I smiled and showed all my pearly whites. I wished my father and I had a close enough relationship to the point of his understanding my body language.
Maybe if he really knew me, he would know that I needed him to save me from the decision I was making.
My feet moved one by one, touching the soft purple petals that highlighted the sequence-of- life carpet. I breathed heavily and tightened my grip.
My father tapped my arm as a reminder that it was time to walk ahead.
He released me and handed me over to my worst enemy.
I knew this man didn't love me, and I didn't love him.
He slowly removed my veil, and with tears in my eyes,
I smiled at the guests and said,
"I do…"

As I Lay

I was there, lying in bed with another man, as my wedding ring brightened the pitch-black room.
I waited for my phone to ring while I was placed in a fetal position by another man pleasing my body.
The sun disappeared in the sky, and our bodies were met by the moon.
My phone still didn't ring, and I changed my position so that I lay on my back.
I wanted to know that my husband cared enough about me to ask about my whereabouts, but hours passed.
My phone never rang.
The man on top of me placed a kiss on my cheek and politely stated,
"Good morning, sunshine. I told you he wasn't the one."

Suicidal Attempts

I attempted suicide on several occasions.
These suicides varied from kitchen knives on my wrist to poisonous friends in my circle.

Life on Repeat

I wanted to grab his attention,
so I was loud.
I wanted to grab his attention,
so I was slutty.
I wanted to grab his attention,
so I was available.
I finally grabbed his attention, and he had his way with me.
I mean, every way possible.
Repeat.

His Mother

I've always hated that lady.
Hate in the sense of hurting so much from disrespect
after I loved her so dearly.
Hate that was created from the soil of despair and watered by years of envy.
Hate that later bloomed from the heat of the sun she had created.

Green Street

I stood in the courtroom, nervous as ever.
I knew what would come from my lips would not be lies, but my defendant intimidated me. She always had that glare in her eyes, and if I saw it, I would need to escape from her trap. I made sure I didn't look to my right. I said, "Your Honor, she is killing herself."
He asked, "Well, who is this 'she' you speak of?"
I took a deep breath and spoke again. "Your Honor, my defendant is killing herself, yet she has so many responsibilities."
I felt my right cheek melt or at least that's how it felt to me.
I knew she was staring. I knew she wanted me to look at her.
I yelled, as if I wanted to get this shit over with, "Your Honor, I would kill for and even die for this woman. She doesn't see how beautiful she is, so she kills herself day by day.
I know she can be strong, because I walk with that strength.
I know she is truly intelligent, because I walk with that knowledge, but Your Honor, she doesn't know herself anymore. She's crying out in the wrong way.
I need your help."
The judge banged his gavel, and as his face turned red, I knew he was pissed.
He shouted to me, "Order in the court! Order in the court! You have to conduct yourself better than this, young lady. Now take a deep breath and speak as if you have some sense."
I wept uncontrollably, and my legs shook.
I looked at my defendant and spoke slowly and softly. The salt from my tears snuck into my mouth as I attempted to move my lips.
I continued, "Your Honor, my mother needs me. She's intentionally doing things to harm herself to get my attention. She won't listen to anything I say, and at times I don't believe she understands how loved she is. Your Honor, please tell my mother I'll give my life for hers if she promises to do better."
I placed my files on the stand, and everything came crashing down.
I looked at the judge, looked at my defendant, and walked out of the courtroom.

Date Rape

I watched my sister get dressed and doll herself up for her special date.
I wondered who this guy was who had made her smile so much over the past few weeks. She came into my room and twirled like a ballerina. She asked me how she looked.
My heart fluttered because in that very moment I saw myself. I watched this eager, loving, self-sufficient being who always loved to live in the moment.
I was awakened out of my blissful daze by a harsh, repetitive noise.
There he was…my sister's date, outside the street, beeping and beeping that damn, loud, elephant-sounding horn.
She begged for me to be nice to this one, so I obliged.
I stepped onto our hard, concrete, broken-down porch stoop, which shared its quarter juice with the local ants.
We waited for the gentleman to step out of his car and approach us, but instead he rolled down the window.
I knew this wasn't a good look for her, but she begged me to let her go.
I kissed her forehead and whispered in her left ear, "My loving you is all you need right now."
I made sure she texted me every hour to talk about my new "brother-in-law," as if they had gone somewhere to elope.
Eleven p.m came, and I couldn't wait to hear from her at twelve.
At midnight I received a call from her cell phone. I was waiting to hear her say she was on her way home, but instead it was a nurse, telling me she was in the hospital, beaten and afraid.

Marriage

I stood there, examining my naked body in the bathroom mirror.
I pulled and tugged on every inch of fat I could find to get
to that beautiful image.
I lifted my hanging breasts under my arms, as if to see how they would look
six inches higher.
I poked my ass out slightly so it would look a little bigger.
I damn near killed myself from squeezing my stomach in for so long.
The next day I found every diet known to man and worked out tirelessly until
I damn near killed myself again.
Then one day I ignored the diets and the workouts.
I introduced my body to my soul, and they are still married to this day.

Transformation

Sacrit

I wanted a different world.
One that didn't judge, one that allowed freedom,
One that saw beauty from within and one that knew the meaning of love,
I wanted a different world,
so I began to live in it.

Soul Cry

I cried for my mother.
She never heard me.
I cried for my father.
He never listened.
I cried for myself.
I found *revolution*.

Perspectives

Life has its way of pissing you off.
One minute you're on top, and the next you're at the very bottom.
Life comes back and asks, "Did you get the message?"
Our misconception of up and down is what had us lost the whole time.

Feminist

I cringed at the thought of being considered the
weakest link in this masculine world.
I later woke up.
I had an overly abundant amount of strength because then I realized they
wouldn't be here if it weren't for a woman like me.

Duty

The first duty for every woman is to herself.
You owe yourself the duty of finding how to live a full, happy life.
It does not matter who you may have to let go to get there, but get there.
It does not matter which job you may have to leave to get there, but get there.
You owe it to yourself to be truthful to yourself, no matter how other people may view your change.
Change when you must. It is your duty.

S & S

Why are we not submissive and subservient when we need to be?
We all should know this has nothing to do with who dominates whom.
Know your position, queen.
And for that you will have your king.
Give to him what he is here to give to you.
When that happens,
your kingdom will always succeed.

Her

She found God the moment she looked in the mirror.
With all three eyes.

S & P

Anything spoken is not of truth.
Truth is silence.
Silence is peace.
Peace is heavenly.

Affirmations

I am the reflection of a strong army. Without my powerful presence, my purpose in this life will not reach its full potential. I walk with strength, knowing that behind me stand billions of women with this same mentality.

I do not exist in a world of demands, betrayal, judgment, or fallacies.
I am living in a world of grants, loyalty, and free will.
I know my energy source allows me to receive only what I put out.

I am not my past hurt!
I am not what they call me!
I am not a bad bitch!
I am not miserable, and I also am not suffering from an inferiority complex.
I am not drowning in pity, nor am I lazy.
I am beautiful. I am healthy. I am a sister, and I am loved

On the next few pages, I ask that you to confess your true emotions right after reading each word. Now that you've read my truths and my stories about overcoming my painful past, I beg you to now become a writer. Be the author of your own story. Write whatever comes to mind. If it's just one word, that's fine, and if you give me a story, I'll be satisfied. Tell me as I told you. If you need to come back and add on, please do just that.

Truth

Beauty

Peace

Fear

Pain

Growth

Love

Sisterhood

Personal Statement

I want to build relationships with the inquisitive souls who've placed their hands on this book. I believe in destiny, and I also believe in unorthodox therapy. After you've completed this book, I would love to continue a relationship with each of you. I believe we can start something powerful between us all.

Twitter - @Nyeeshad
Instagram - @Nyeeshad
Direct Email – Nyeesha@sacritdevas.org

www.ingramcontent.com/pod-product-compliance
Lightning Source LLC
Chambersburg PA
CBHW050647160426
43194CB00010B/1840